Jesus Others You

The Self-Centered Gospel

By
Joshua Banks

WESTBOW
PRESS®
A DIVISION OF THOMAS NELSON
& ZONDERVAN

Photography provided by Hammondovi
Graphic Design provided by GraphixMain

All scripture references used are from The Holy Bible, King James Version, New International Version, New American Standard and Message Versions.

This book is a work of non-fiction. Unless otherwise noted, the author and the publisher make no explicit guarantees as to the accuracy of the information contained in this book and in some cases, names of people and places have been altered to protect their privacy.

WestBow Press books may be ordered through booksellers or by contacting:

WestBow Press
A Division of Thomas Nelson & Zondervan
1663 Liberty Drive
Bloomington, IN 47403
www.westbowpress.com
1 (866) 928-1240

ISBN: 978-1-5127-5748-4 (sc)
ISBN: 978-1-5127-5749-1 (e)

Print information available on the last page.

WestBow Press rev. date: 9/23/2016

Special Thanks
The Banks Family,
Felicia Murray,
Isaac Rowe.

About the Author

Joshua Banks has been involved in ministry since the age of 15, serving in several capacities of leadership from Youth Worship team leader to Discipleship group leader to Young Adult pastor. Throughout his years of service, he has gained valuable training and insights into his personal relationship with God, the church, and the various dynamics of the relationship between the church and the congregants.

A 2003 graduate of Rhema Bible College in Tulsa, Oklahoma, Joshua's graduating class was the last to receive great tutelage in the college setting from the late Kenneth Hagin, Sr. After graduation, he entered the field of law enforcement where he spent nine years serving the Travis County Sheriff's Office in Austin, Texas. During his tenure, he received numerous awards in recognition of his excellent work. He is most proud of being recognized for his service to his community.

Joshua can be contacted via email at
SelfCenteredGospel@gmail.com

Follow me on Twitter:
JoshuaBanksAuthor@JBanksAuthor

Or on Facebook:
Author Joshua Banks

TABLE OF CONTENTS

Introduction

My life has been, like most lives, filled with challenges and discoveries. With every season and change comes a new understanding of old concepts and ways of thinking; along with that, enters an opportunity to change what we choose to believe about those ways of thinking and concepts.

One of these moments of discovery for me came when I was able to recognize that there was a difference between being "Churchlike" and becoming Christ-like. The idea of being "churchlike" is much like the saying, "When in Rome, do as the Romans do". In our circles, we did what we knew was expected of us: sing when it's time to sing, sit or stand on cue. An occasional, "Amen" or nodding of the head affirms your support and agreement with what is being said. And of course nothing displays the authenticity of your faith more than your regular, and sometimes sacrificial, financial support. Eventually, you achieved the image of being a good, respected Christian. Most of us experience a performance-based form of Christianity customized to the cultures of our particular churches.

Sadly, enough, the Sunday morning routine is the most spiritual thing that some people experience all week. Others will take it a step further and allow their faith to impact their moral standards. The Bible becomes our *Basic instruction before leaving earth*, sort of a rule book to guarantee an eternity in heaven. This is not to say that what we do or have done has not been authentic or heartfelt, but one must ask the question, "Is there more?"

To the true seeker, the image and accolade of being a good, respected Christian is not enough. The true seeker demands for a personal experience—to know Christ, to be like Christ, and to be transformed from the inside out.

Through a series of scripture and personal revelation, I want us to explore the importance of discovering our unique God-given blueprints, rather than relying solely on the feedback from external sources, such as church, friends, or even family. We go to the Word to examine what God and Jesus really had to say about individuality, and what comes first: others, or the self. We will take a look at what God says about Himself, and how that relates to our own design.

As we take this journey together, I ask you to open up your mind to the possibility of having a deeper connection with God and a better understanding of yourself.

CULTURAL OBSERVATION

As the son of a pastor, most of my early life was spent within the four walls of the church. I have fond memories of participating in a wide range of activities; from feeding the homeless and visiting nursing homes, to performing in plays, dramas, and musical activities there was always something to do and somewhere to be involved. I quickly learned that spending a substantial amount of time in any environment exposes you to the particular culture of that environment.

Church culture is, indeed, a culture all on its own complete with its own language, protocol, class system, etc. Now, of course, the message that we would proclaim was always that of, "Come one, come all. Everyone is equal and welcomed here." But somewhere between the lines of that mantra, it was obvious that some people and activities did not flow as well, or feel so openly inviting, in our Church Culture.

This type of culture is not necessarily taught upfront. While it is a given that churches will spell out their Tenants of Faith and the doctrines that they identify as foundational to their message, those proclamations do not necessarily define the culture. The people who occupy an environment are just as responsible, if not more responsible, for defining the culture of that environment as much as it would be with any established principles or set of rules.

Merriam-Webster's(n.d.) online dictionary defines "culture" as, "the beliefs, customs, arts, etc., of a particular society, group, place, or time." Perhaps even more specific to the conversation at hand is the third definition offered by Webster, "a way of thinking, behaving, or working that exists in a place or organization." Over time, when a culture is established, both definitions can be summed up in the phrase, "Well, this is just how we do it here." This reality is not necessarily a bad thing. There are many benefits to the particular cultures that exist within our churches or social organizations.

It would be foolish to assume that every person occupying our churches (congregants, pulpits, positions of leadership) have "got it all together". It is in fact quite the opposite; most of us don't have it all together. The church is made up of all kinds of people from all walks of life, with their own unique differences and levels of both secular and biblical education. We are joined together by our common need for a Savior and our desire to fashion our lives after His teachings.

It is this understanding of culture and who it is that establishes the culture that caused me to ask a lot of questions--- questions like, "Why are we doing that," "Who said this was wrong/right," "Where did we get that idea from," and my favorite question "Is that even Biblical?"

Let me pause for a moment and say, just because certain activities are not biblical, does not make them wrong. Many times we do things because they are enjoyable to the members of our community. Some church communities prefer to be more traditional in their styles of worship and appearance, while other church communities prefer a more laid back modern approach to dress and styles of worship. Hymns or ballads, pews or chairs, pipe organs or electric guitars, neither is more right or wrong than the other. The beautiful thing about any particular culture is its ability to allow for various unique forms of expression.

It becomes very easy sometimes to get locked into a legalistic way of doing things that suppresses our God-given individuality. I believe that the worst thing we could ever do with the Bible is reduce it down to a set of laws that need to be executed to the letter. The primary purpose of scripture is to introduce us to God for the sake of developing a personal relationship. From an authentic, personal relationship comes an authentic expression of love and worship.

In observing the culture of our churches in general, we will find that many times "good" ideas are taught, passed down and enforced rather than *God* ideas. It is in a similar vein of thought that Jesus said to the Teachers of His day:

> "...*And by this* you invalidated the word of God for the sake of your tradition. You hypocrites, rightly did Isaiah prophesy of you, saying: 'This people honors Me with their lips, but their heart is far away from Me. 'But in vain

do they worship Me, Teaching as doctrines the precepts of men" (Matthew 15:6-9 New American Standard Bible).

Do we at times cut off the life that should come with the truth of God's word because of our own cultural traditions, practices, and social expectations? How much of what we teach as Doctrine finds its roots more in good sounding ideas rather than in the Word of God itself? How much of our culture and traditions that we mandate and enforce, are based more on preference than principle? While I understand that many times we do the best we can with the information and resources available to us, it would do us all some good to take a step back and observe the culture in our communities of faith. What impact does our enforced culture have on the people who come into our churches for healing and wholeness?

When I say "enforced culture," I am referring to the legalistic, preference-based standards that we enforce on our congregants. Whether it is the length of a skirt, the smoking of a cigarette or the different styles of music that we approve or disapprove of, most church cultures each have their own signature brand of an "enforced culture."

You see there is a danger in our church cultures to be aware of. Because we don't have it all together, many times we can teach things from a place of pain and unresolved personal hurts, that does more harm to people than it does to help them. In this method, personal experiences can be taught as concrete spiritual revelation; likewise, personal convictions can become like laws for everyone to adhere to.

Growing up, one of the teachings that was a part of the culture in a couple of the Christian communities I was a part of was the acronym JOY: Jesus first, Others second and Yourself last.

I would assume that this way of thinking, or this particular acronym is something that most Christians can identify with. There is however something incomplete and perhaps wrong with this way of thinking. While I realize that I just opened up a can of worms, I ask that before you write me off as one majoring on minors; consider the implications of such a pious sounding statement.

I would never dispute any principle that focuses on Jesus being first. Philippians tells us that God exalted Jesus to the highest place and gave Him the name that is above every name. That at the name of Jesus every knee should bow, in heaven and on earth and under the earth, and every tongue confess that Jesus Christ is Lord. (Phil. 2:10-12). Again and again the Bible teaches us that Jesus is Lord. He is first. The part that comes next in the acronym is what I found to be somewhat misleading.

Are we really to think of Jesus first and then follow up that thought with our concern for the needs of others, and once we've seen to the needs of those around us, then and only then are we to consider ourselves? I say NO! I believe that the scripture also opposes this order of priorities.

A SELF-CENTERED GOSPEL?

Many of us would shudder at such the seemingly heretical statement "a self-centered gospel".

It is said that the most important part of any conversation is a shared definition of terms. We have to agree, or at least become familiar, with the terminology being used in order to have a proper understanding of what is really being said.

After hearing a term like *Self-Centered*, I know that some of your minds immediately interpret that to mean *selfish*. I'd like to clearly differentiate between the two terms.

Merriam-Webster's online dictionary (n.d.) defines *selfish* as "lacking consideration for others; concerned chiefly with one's own personal profit or pleasure". To understand what *Self-Centered* really means we must break down each word individually. *Self* is defined as "a person's essential being that distinguishes them from others, especially considered as the object of introspection or reflexive action." *Centered* is defined as "placed or situated in the center; having the specified subject as the focal element." When placed together, we see that a self-centered individual places what is at their core as the top priority in decision making. This prioritizing does not disregard others, nor is it necessarily about profit or pleasure, rather authenticity.

Be patient with me as I attempt to show how being Self-Centered is how we are created and designed to exist.

Our cultures shape the way that we view not only ourselves and the world around us, but the way we view God. It has been my experience that the majority of my beliefs about God came from being in different church cultures, not necessarily from the Word of God or my relationship with Him. It was not until I began to look in the scriptures for myself, outside of the constraints of any cultural bias, that I began to notice characteristics of God that I had not been aware of.

I grew up learning about the supremacy of God. I was taught at a young age about God's omnipotence, omniscience and omnipresent qualities. I was well aware of God being love. All of these truths about God were things that would be accepted by most believers. It was not until I read Isaiah 43:25 that I found God challenging my beliefs. It states, "I, even I, am He who blots out your transgressions for My own sake; and I will not remember your sins." (NKJV)

When I read this scripture, the question came to me, "For whose sake did God forgive their sins and blot out their transgressions?" One would think that a scripture such as this would read more along the lines of a John 3:16 and place the source of His forgiveness on His never-ending love. This is not the case. God is forgiving sins for His sake, for His pleasure. God did it because He wanted to.

In Genesis, we see God creating everything that is in the universe. We see the pattern established where God creates something; God evaluates what He creates and compliments the beauty of His own creations.

Being a musical composer, I often look at the body of music that I come up with, and I judge the product by what seems good to me. If I like it, I say that its good and I keep it. If I do not like it, I say that it is not good and I discard it. I understand that not everyone composes music; but everyone, at some point or another, has probably watched someone bake a cake. They add each ingredient and occasionally they stick their spoon in the batter to taste it. One of my favorite memories as a kid was waiting for my mom to make cookies or a cake so that I would be able to lick the spoon whenever she was finished. Mmm Mmm! If the cook felt that more sugar was needed, more sugar was added. Things were mixed and stirred until the one preparing it looked back and said, "Ah that's it!"

In the same way, God evaluated His own handiwork, and placed His own seal of approval on each item He had created. God said that it was good. Another way of saying this would be, God liked it. Who is it that sets the standard of what is good in the sight of God? He does. He makes things the way He likes them. He forgives sins because that is what He wants to do. It pleases Him to do so. His nature is Goodness. This leads to an interesting conclusion: God does things because it feels good to *Him*. God is an introspective being.

He looks inside of Himself. He operates from a place of "Oneness." James 1:7 says, "Every good gift and every perfect gift is from above, coming down from the Father of the lights, with whom can be no variation, neither shadow that is cast by turning" (American Standard Version). I explain, "...no variation, neither shadow that is cast by turning" to mean that there is no division within Him, nor is there any deviation from His original thought or idea. His "Yes" is His "Yes".

Perhaps it is hard for us to see God using this process. The Bible says that we are created in the image and likeness of GOD. Are we truly created as introspective beings, designed to look inside of our hearts and spirits in the same way God does, and do the things that make us feel good? Perhaps you may be questioning the whole premise that I am presenting because it seems presumptuous to state that God would look inside of Himself. After all, He's God. He is not divided in the way that we are spirit, soul, and body. What is clear is that God is Spirit. God operates from that realm. While we could debate back and forth whether or not God would need to look "inside," what is not debatable is the fact that God chose to leave an example for us to walk out our divine nature. For us, this means that we have to follow the example left by God, Himself and operate from the realm of the Spirit. Jesus very clearly stated, "For out of the overflow of the heart the mouth speaks. The good man brings good things out of the good stored up in him, and the evil man brings evil things out of the evil stored up in him" (Matthew 12:34-35 NIV). Paul also said "Yet we have the same spirit of faith as he had who wrote, I have believed, and therefore have I spoken. We too believe, and therefore we speak" (2 Corinthians 4:13 Amplified Version). To sum it up, God lives from the inside out.

I realize that all kinds of wild hairs may have just been raised. I mean, who ever heard of doing things outwardly, because it agrees with us and pleases us inwardly/spiritually? We are created to live in this way, as God does, from the inside out.

INSIDE OUT

Proverbs 23:7 says, "For as he thinks in his heart, so is he" (NKJV). The outward expression of a man's life is determined by his own inward thoughts and perceptions, whether he intends for it to be this way or not. If deep down on the inside you believe that you are a failure, then you will find that failure seems to find you no matter where you go or what you endeavor to accomplish. Not only that, but if you believe that you are a failure inwardly, every outward manifestation of failure that takes place in your life, will be met with a sense of inward agreement. You'll find an excuse and a reason to justify every failure that takes place in your life. No matter how much you hate it, it will agree with a part of you, the part that believes you are a failure. It will be as if you had expected to fail.

Now would be a good time to stop and reflect on the condition of your life. It becomes so easy to blame situations on other people, but based on the scripture, *our hearts* set the stage for the issues of our lives. What is in your heart? How have your inward belief systems whether consciously or subconsciously affected the quality of your life? This is not to say that our lives are not impacted by the decisions of others that are sometimes beyond our control, but whenever we choose to be a victim of our pasts or the decisions of others, we ignore our own personal responsibility to change;

we underestimate our own internal strength to rise above circumstances.

Earlier we referred to 2 Corinthians 4:13 which states, "It is written: "I believed; therefore, I have spoken" (NIV) and Romans 10:9 which says that we are to confess with our mouth the thing that we already believe in our heart.

Perhaps you have heard the saying, "my word is my bond," or a reference to the "good old days" when a man's handshake was all that was needed to ratify any agreement. This way of thinking describes a culture in which it was recognized that an outward form of expression, whether by word or by deed, was a reflection of your inward convictions and commitments. Jesus told his disciples, "Simply let your 'Yes' be 'Yes,' and your 'No,' 'No'; anything beyond this comes from the evil one" (Matthew 5:37 NIV). Jesus is explaining an "inside out" way of living. If on the inside your decision is either yes or no, and you are committed to that decision then let your outward response reflect your inward decision.

For example, do you have that one friend that every time they call you, they want something or need something? You see their number and you already know that, whatever this call is about, it's probably going to cost you your time or your money or both. You answer the phone knowing what's about to happen, and within minutes you've signed yourself up to help run a series of errands that just so happens to take place on your only off day. You get to your off-day and as you're running around playing chauffeur, you can only think about how mad you are at yourself for agreeing to this. Instead of being glad that you're able to help, you're inwardly beating yourself up because everything inside of you was screaming "No" and yet you gave an outward "Yes."

This particular point has been one of the places in which I disagree with how many teach the principle of confessing the Word of God in order to receive from God. It is taught that one is to confess (audibly) scriptures that apply to your situation in order to see your situation change and begin to reflect what the Bible says about your situation. For example, if you are experiencing sickness in your body, you should find a scripture that refers to the healing power of God, and then confess (audibly speak) the scripture over your body until your body manifests the healing. Scriptures like Isaiah 53:5 become repetitive clichés that get thrown around as if they were some type of magic charm that demand results if you say it enough times. While I don't believe that this is an altogether false teaching, I believe it is incomplete.

The Bible emphasizes an inside out way of thinking and living. We are not speaking things with our mouth for the purpose of believing it in our heart; we believe it in our hearts first, and from the overflow of belief, we are able to boldly confess it from our mouth. Sincere confession always displays what exists in the heart.

If we do not believe something on the inside, to verbalize it on the outside would be a lie. When

God calls things that "Be not as though they were," He is doing so from a place of confidence. He is convinced inwardly that everything He says outwardly will absolutely and always happen (Isaiah 55:11).

We are all guilty of speaking things that we do not believe. It is akin to our culture. We are all familiar with the standard greeting, "How are you doing today?" with the typical response of "I'm fine. How are you?" How many times have you said that out of habit rather than sincerity? How many times do we say that we are "fine" knowing that all our lives are spinning out of control?

We have grown so accustomed to saying things that we don't believe; it's no wonder that so many have little to no results in our application of the Word. We speak vain repetitions hoping to build our faith with things we don't believe. What we need is to give people a reason to believe. Put the emphasis on what it is about those scriptures that supports the belief that we need to hold on to. Faith is a result of hearing and believing what the Word of God has to say. God told Joshua, "Do not let this Book of the Law depart from your mouth; meditate on it day and night, so that you may be careful to do everything written in it. Then you will be prosperous and successful." (Joshua 1:8 NIV)

In order to receive the benefits of any type of medication, the medicine must do more than just be placed inside of one's mouth. The full benefits are not experienced until the body absorbs the medication. Medications are biological and must be absorbed into the appropriate cells. In the same way that lotion is not just applied to the skin, but is rubbed in so that it can be absorbed. We too must do more than just apply the word to our mouths. We need to let it be absorbed into our whole being. In doing so, we can speak outwardly from a place of inward conviction.

The conversation of inside out living and confessing of the Word requires that at some point, we take an inventory of our inward beliefs. In order for us to speak what we believe, we need to identify what it is that we truly believe. This is not always easy, but if anything is true about successful living, it is that it is done on purpose. We need to take ownership of our beliefs, and if need be, change those beliefs so that our outward confessions agree with our inward convictions.

Earlier I asked the question, are we truly created as introspective beings that are designed to look inside in the same way God does, and do the things that makes us feel good. We have discussed how we are designed to be introspective and live from the inside out, but what about the part about doing what feels good? Feelings can be a dangerous guide. Jeremiah 17:9 reads, "The heart is deceitful above all things and beyond cure. Who can understand it?" (NIV).

According to *Strong's Concordance*, the word used here for "heart" is the Hebrew word "Leb." James Strong defines Leb as "the heart; also used (figuratively) very widely for the feelings, the will and even the intellect; likewise, for the center

17

of anything." Feelings are deceptive and fickle. The heart is an unsteady guide, but according to Proverbs, it is the most important factor in the position and placement of our lives. Proverbs 4:23, "Above all else, guard your heart, for everything you do flows from it" (NIV).

"Above all else." This is not any mere suggestion but something that is absolutely essential. The Bible tells us that the most important thing for us to do is to guard our hearts which, as we saw earlier, refers to the intangible parts of us, including our feelings. As any guard posted outside of the White House monitors who are allowed access to the facilities, we are to apply the same diligence to the things that we allow access to our hearts. Listen to what Jesus had to say about the heart; "The good man brings good things out of the good stored up in his heart, and the evil man brings evil things out of the evil stored up in his heart. For out of the overflow of his heart his mouth speaks" (Luke 6:45 NIV).

The overflow of your heart, determines the type of person that you are. Jesus also said, "But whatever comes out of the mouth comes from the heart, and this is what makes a man unclean and defiles [him]." (Matthew 15:18 Amplified Bible, Classic Edition).

We are born in a fallen condition. We have our hearts already set out to do the things that do not please God before we are even confronted with an opportunity to make a decision, until we wake up to the truth.

God said in Ezekiel 36:26 that he would give us a new heart with a new spirit. With this new heart comes a new nature. Our spirit is merged with His spirit. In Galatians 5:22, we learn the fruits of this spiritual merger. Our old heart and nature is absolutely untrustworthy, and so one of the greatest gifts that God ever gave us, was the ability to have the inward leading that comes by His spirit merging with our spirit.

To the recreated heart, the things that will feel good on the inside will be the things that come from the fruit listed in Galatians 5:22. The leading of the spirit brings about an inward peace that confirms the things that God speaks to us through His word. Like our Creator, we are created to look inwardly and to move and flow based upon what it is that comes out of us. With this type of foundation in place, I will move on the next point.

Several years ago I was challenged with a thought that the Bible teaches a "self before others" type of Gospel. This thought was totally contradictory to what most of us were taught, but I felt that God was leading me to observe some things from a scriptural perspective that seemed to be out of place, of course a result of our church culture.

If learning about God's "for Mine own sake" motivated forgiveness was the first step down what seemed to be a different understanding of who God was, Matthew 22:37-40 would have been the second and even more thought-provoking step. It states, "Jesus replied: "'Love the Lord your God with all your heart and with all your soul and with all your mind.' This is the first and greatest commandment. And the second is like it: 'Love your neighbor as yourself.' All the Law and the Prophets hang on these two commandments" (NIV).

Jesus was asked the question, "Which commandment is the greatest?" Jesus was being asked to take all of the Jewish laws and give His insight as to which one of them was the absolute greatest. Jesus' answer is a passage that is common among churches and Christians all over, however, I feel that while we have all committed this verse to memory, few of us have really looked at what it was that Jesus said.

The first answer He gives is to love God, which would easily be the J of the JOY acronym, but what was the second? Jesus says the second is like the first. How is it like the first? It is like the first because it is crucially important. Jesus says that the second is to love your neighbor as yourself.

Every time that I can recall, when I hear this verse used, the emphasis is on the loving of one's neighbor, and it's from this type of thinking that we develop our acronym. But Jesus said to love your neighbor "as" or "in the same way" that you love yourself.

Our teachings, sermons and messages focus so much on how we should love other people and very little on how we love ourselves. Most of the people around us can do a great job of doing something for someone else but are very poor at doing beneficial things for themselves. Now we know how to pamper ourselves with new clothes and jewelry; we are professionals at making masks for ourselves that make us appear to have everything together. We can hide behind our status, or our wealth, but the tragic truth is that most of us are masters at loving God, proficient in loving others and terrible at loving ourselves. It is this sense of self-contempt that causes a man to take his internal fight and manifest it to the world as a hard, cold shell---one that appears to be immune to pain and emotion. It is this low sense of self-worth that causes for a young lady to offer up her body to multiple lovers, desperately wanting to be desired and loved. The same would be true of a man who would prefer the cheap thrills of loose living, rather than prefer the benefits that come from true commitment.

We move from one high to the next high, suppressing the inward screams with more and more things to distract us from the truth, the truth that most of us have no idea how to love ourselves. If we do not know how to love ourselves, what kind of love is it that we have been giving our neighbors?

We have been making charges of love to an account that has insufficient funds to cover those charges. Consequently, we give people a fabricated form of love that lacks the ability to produce the type of fruits that love should be producing. Fruits like love, joy, peace, forbearance, kindness, goodness, faithfulness, gentleness, and self-control. (Galatians 5:22-23)

SELFLESS ACTIONS?

Have you ever heard anyone say how they feel like they sacrifice so much for others, and no one appreciates their sacrifices? How much of our time is spent investing in others only to leave us feeling unappreciated, empty, and undervalued?

I observe what appears to be a fallacy in the philosophy of what we call *self-less acts*. Usually we consider what we do for someone else, something that we don't particularly enjoy, as a "selfless act." The word in itself broken apart---self-less---implies that the only one who benefitted from your act of service was the one for whom the service or sacrifice was performed. I submit for your consideration, there are no such things as self-less acts. Everything that we choose to do, at some level no matter how deeply we may bury it inside of ourselves, causes us to experience some type of gratification.

The mother that sacrifices all of her time and energy cooking and cleaning doesn't make all of her sacrifices exclusively for the sake of her children, as she may profess. She does it because in her heart, she has an image of what it is to be a good mother. Her outward actions then come into alignment with her inward convictions. It is in this that she finds satisfaction. She is willing to suffer sleepless nights and endless trips back and forth fulfilling the needs of her children because of this needed internal agreement that is inside of us all.

Most of us are too busy to notice this truth, and even more of us don't love ourselves enough to spend the time evaluating the depth of what it is that truly motivates our words, thoughts and actions.

Perhaps an awareness of this thought might prove liberating to the individual who feels like their sacrifices go unappreciated. They don't--- they are appreciated and valuable to you.

The danger involved in the philosophy of selfless actions, is that this thinking trains the mind to disassociate ourselves from the actions we participate in. It subtly tricks us into believing that we can separate who we are from what we do, when in reality, what we do is a result of who we are. This philosophy robs us of the inward reward that comes from inside-out living. Ultimately you will always find yourself dependent on external validation, when in fact your commitment to what is on the inside of you can provide a validation all by itself.

Think of the way you feel after you know that you have done your best and seen success. That feeling of satisfaction that you get when you set a goal for yourself, fought off the temptation to quit, and finally see yourself achieving the goal that you set for yourself.

Going back to our example of the mother who sacrifices so much for her children, think of the great joy she feels as her children grow and develop into productive people because of the countless lessons and examples she has poured into them. Proverbs 31:28 says, referring to such a woman, "Her children rise up and call her blessed; her husband also, and he praises her". (English Standard Version). Because of her *inside out* way of living, those affected by who she *is* identify her as *blessed.* In essence, we should seek internal agreement as much as we pursue public affirmation.

Additionally, Proverbs 31:30 says, "Give her of the fruit of her hands, and let her works praise her in the gates" (ESV). The 'fruit' of her hands, which are the countless hours and sacrifices she has made for her children, turn around and praise her. Who she *is*, determines what she *does*, then what she does, when seen through the eyes of others, publicly confirms who she was all along.

I am not saying that we do not *need* words of affirmation or external praise. I am saying that we should learn how to love ourselves and see the value in what we do because that is authentically who we are.

Most modern psychotherapists will agree that loving yourself is not an event, it is a process. It is something that takes work. It requires us to be more introspective than what most of us are willing to be. Learning how to love ourselves gives us the freedom to be our True Self.

In an article written in Psychology Today, psychotherapists Ken Page writes:

"As much as we want to control our own destiny, the humbling truth is that sometimes the only way to learn self-love is by BEING loved---precisely in the places where we feel most unsure and most tender. When that happens, we feel freedom and relief---and permission to love in a deeper way. No amount of positive self-talk can replicate this experience. It is a gift of intimacy, not of will-power" (Page, 2011)

What a powerful statement! It is a statement like this that perfectly explains the essence behind the greatest commandment. In loving God with all that is inside of us, He is able to love the parts of us that we feel are unlovable. He is able to cleanse the parts that we feel are beyond cleansing. It is from this position of intimacy that we experience, within our love affair with the God who is love, that we are able to be filled with His love. It is through constant communion with Him that we are filled with His love. Out of the abundance of love for Him, we are able to love ourselves the way that He loves us. From this position of self-love, we are able to love the world.

For most of us, the gifts given to us from God lay dormant inside of us, never having been touched or developed. Those of us who are serious about loving others without loving ourselves would be wise to listen to the words of Paul to Timothy in 1Timothy 4:11-14. Paul along with other instruction tells Timothy to not neglect the gift that was imparted to him. Paul then goes on in verses 15 and 16 to say, "Be diligent in these matters; give yourself wholly to them, so that everyone may see your progress. Watch your life and doctrine closely. Persevere in them, because if you do, you will save both yourself and your hearers" (1 Tim 4:15-16 NIV).

Paul told Timothy that the salvation of not only himself, but also all around him depended on his awareness of his gift. Could it be that one of the greatest ways to love our neighbor is to develop ourselves?

In the book of Romans, Paul encouraged the church at Rome by saying:

"For by the grace given me I say to every one of you: Do not think of yourself more highly than you ought, but rather think of yourself with sober judgment, in accordance with the measure of faith God has given you. Just as each of us has one body with many members, and these members do not all have the same function, so in Christ we who are many form one body, and each member belongs to all the others. We have different gifts, according to the grace given us. If a man's gift is prophesying, let him use it in proportion to his faith. If it is serving, let him serve; if it is teaching, let him teach; if it is encouraging, let him encourage; if it is contributing to the needs of others, let him give generously; if it is leadership, let him govern diligently; if it is showing mercy, let him do it cheerfully" (Rom 12:3-8 NIV).

Paul's next words to the Church of Rome are "Love must be sincere" (Rom 12:9 NIV). Could it be that the sincerity of our love is in direct connection to seeing ourselves with a sober judgment and giving our gifts to others? What is a sober judgment? It is a balanced accurate judgment. For most of us, a sober judgment of ourselves would actually cause us to see ourselves as more than what we currently allow ourselves to see. There are those who think more highly of themselves but usually an arrogant person exaggerates their better qualities to keep you distracted from their deep insecurities. In contrast, a sober judgment is one that allows you to assess your strengths and weakness, with honesty, and provides you a confidence in being who you were created to be.

Paul says, "Make a careful exploration of who you are and the work you have been given, and then sink yourself into that. Don't be impressed with yourself. Don't compare yourself with others. Each of you must take responsibility for doing the creative best you can with your own life. (Gal. 6: 4-5, The Message)

How much time do you spend developing yourself? When was the last time that you invested in yourself? When was the last time that you spent time with yourself getting to know who you are? How much value do you place on your own opinion or perspective?

Still not sold on this whole Jesus-You-Others thing? I've got one more passage of scripture for you to consider. Galatians 6 states, "Brethren, if a man is overtaken in any trespass, you who are spiritual restore such a one in a spirit of gentleness, considering yourself lest you also be tempted. Bear one another's burdens, and so fulfill the law of Christ. For if anyone thinks himself to be something, when he is nothing, he deceives himself. But let each one examine his own work, and then he will have rejoicing in himself alone, and not in another. For each one shall bear his own load" (Gal 6:1-5 NKJV).

Paul's instruction was that we should be quick and willing to help those who fall with the thought in mind, "How would I want others to treat me if I were caught in a temptation?" Paul says that in doing this, we fulfill the Law of Christ...and which law would that be? The exact law that instructs us to love our neighbors as we love ourselves.

A PLACE OF ONENESS

I have seen many people both in the church and outside of the church suffer because they failed to take the time to see the deeper value in themselves. They spend their whole lives masking their true selves and selling people the self that they think others want to see. The Son has come to set us free, free to be everything He created us to be.

Are we to honor and give preference to others? There is absolutely a time for that, but more importantly we have a responsibility to become intimate with Jesus. Allow ourselves to be loved in every area of our lives so that He can heal us. He can take our darkest parts and make them beautiful and bright for His glory, but there is more to this story.

When Jesus walked the Earth, one of the things that Jesus did, much to the irritation of the religious leaders of His time, was make it very clear that He was one with the Father. Same in Spirit, same in essence, perfectly synchronized in thought and deed. If there's anything that Jesus knew, He knew of His positioning with the Father, as they were one. One of the things I used to teach to one of my college Bible groups was that God never asks us to do something that He is not willing to do or has not already done Himself. Many times when we see the examples of how Jesus lived, we tend to excuse His action away because after all "That's Jesus and He was God", but when we choose to see Jesus as being on another level, it is to our own detriment.

Jesus stripped Himself of His Deity and was a man. He lived as a man, He thought as a man, being filled with the Spirit, but I believe that the most important thing in Jesus' life was the revelation of who He was *in the Father*. It was this revelation that placed Him in a position of confidence that was unshakable. Jesus never did anything outwardly that did not agree with what His spirit was telling Him inwardly. He knew that His spirit was joined with the very Spirit of the Father. When He spoke, it was what the Father spoke; when he acted, it was mirrored after the Father (John 5:19)

Would it be possible for us to have this same type of relationship with the Father? Listen to the words of Ephesians 2:18: "For through Him we both have access to the Father by one Spirit" (NIV). Because of Christ, we share the same Spirit that Jesus and the Father share. We are one. I have direct and instant access to God. My spirit is connected to Him.

With the thought of this oneness that we share with Jesus and the Father, as it relates to our acronym, we are in the *J* of the *JOY*. We are in Jesus. We are one with Him. That connection causes us to experience the peace and love that is necessary for our hearts to develop and our true self to emerge. It is from this abundance of love and the emergence of our true selves that we are able to love the world the way that we are loved. In this love, we can provide the world with something pure and genuine.

Many of us will not readily accept this thought---the thought of us being in an intimate relationship with God that results in us sharing the same type of oneness with the Father that Jesus Himself shares. Our minds tend to reject this type of a notion. I know that in my own personal life, this revelation was a difficult one to wrap my mind around. But why is this so difficult for us to accept?

While most of us would sit in a pew, hear of us being "In Christ" from the pulpit, and nod our heads in agreement, deep down inside we are still waiting to be convinced. News like this seems almost too good to be true. What is it that hinders us from jumping head first into this revelation?

Now if you're like me, your mind has a quick response to this answer: sin. We see ourselves as sinful, saved or not. We see our faults and failures. We see how far short we've come to meeting the standards of excellence and perfection that a holy God would demand.

I remember hearing again and again about the Holiness of God. I remember being told that it is man's sinful nature that separates him from a holy God. I remember hearing about how sin could not stand in the presence of a holy and pure God. How easy it is for us to remember that we have all sinned; after all, nobody is perfect except for God. It is this constant focusing on the power of sin that we willingly walk away from the power of God.

Allow me to say something that will challenge your way of thinking. God can handle your sin. God hates sin, this is true, but unlike what some of us have been taught to believe; God does not separate Himself from sinners.

Think back to the Garden of Eden in the book of Genesis. Adam and Eve disobey God's commands; they eat from the Tree of the Knowledge of Good and Evil and immediately realize that they are naked. Sin consciousness instantly took over, causing them to feel ashamed but here's the part that gets overlooked. An all knowing, all seeing, omnipresent God, shows up in the same place that He always shows up to meet with the ones He loved. He knew what they did, and He showed up anyway! Did He judge them for their sins? Yes. But why would He show up and call for them if He was so repulsed by the sin in them?

If you look at the life of Abraham, here is a man who clearly gets it wrong plenty of times, yet in all of this, God continues to show up and speak to him face to face. What about Jacob, the liar and trickster, who wrestles with God all night? Consider Samson, the man who wakes up from Delilah's bed and the Spirit of God instantly falls on Him. Not only can God handle being in the presence of sinful people, in the book of Job, He calls Satan into His throne room and has a conversation with him about Job.

What am I trying to prove? We have been taught more about the power of sin and the great distance we are from the mark of God, that we forget something about the character of God. Isaiah states, "Therefore the Lord himself will give you a sign: The virgin will be with child and will give birth to a son, and will call him Immanuel" (Isaiah 7:14 NIV).

I STILL SEE YOU

The name, Immanuel, is so profound. The revelation of its meaning has absolutely changed the way I think about God. Immanuel means "God with us." Although I have known this definition for as long as I can remember, the magnitude of its meaning had never dawned on me until recently. God with us. Not God over here or God over there. Not God with me whenever I make Him happy. Not God with me only when I do the right things, but God with me right here, right now. The author of Psalms 139 makes this fact crystal clear when he writes:

> "Where could I go from Your Spirit? Or where could I flee from Your presence? If I ascend up into heaven, You are there; if I make my bed in Sheol (the place of the dead), behold, You are there. If I take the wings of the morning or dwell in the uttermost parts of the sea, even there shall Your hand lead me, and Your right hand shall hold me" (Ps 139:7-10 AMP).

If you have never read that passage of scripture, I highly recommend that you read it and allow it to become as familiar to you as John 3:16 because God is absolutely with us. He will never leave us nor forsake us.

I cannot begin to count the times that I've been in the wrong place, with the wrong people, and heard God speak to me. I remember the first time that happened, it shocked me. I was thinking, "Wait a minute, what are you doing in here?" It seems comical, but when you really think about it, we act as if the things we do or the things we have done take God by surprise. Then, in shame, we pull away from God and allow the consciousness of our own sins to cause us to pull an "Adam and Eve", hiding ourselves in the bushes.

Can you imagine how silly we look to God when we allow ourselves to cower away from Him in guilt and shame? It reminds me of when a small child covers their own eyes and then says to their watching parents, "Mommy, Daddy, you can't see me." The parent lovingly responds, "I can still see you." The child then picks the most ridiculous of hiding spots, to which the parent responds, "I still see you". God is right here with us saying to us, *I still see you. I still want you.* The offer for oneness is still extended not because of how good you are, but because of how good He is.

Don't allow the knowledge of your failures to keep you from realizing the oneness you have with God through Jesus. The judgment that God had in a response to sin, He poured it on Jesus. He poured it all on Jesus.

One of the things that helped me accept and recognize the great love of God, was when God revealed to me what the Greek word *Agape'* really was.

The New Testament was translated from Greek to Latin and eventually English. As with any translation from one language to another, some of the original meaning of any word can be lost. In the English language, we use the word "love" to describe how we feel about a diverse body of subjects: food, our possessions, and one another. You can love fried chicken while also loving your car and its cool, new features with the same word you use with your sweetheart when you say, "I love you, baby", however in the Greek language, there are words to describe each use of the word, "love." The kind of love that God has is referred to as *Agape'*. It is this type of love that is never ending, never failing; this is the love that He put inside of us when our spirit joined with His. (Romans 5:5)

On my way to celebrate my birthday several years ago, God revealed to me that, "Loving the way I love, means recognizing and loving the God-signature in another individual." Now, when I heard that, it didn't make much sense to me, but as I meditated upon it more and more, I realized that God sees Himself in us. We were created that way: in His image and likeness. Every time He looks at you and me, He sees Himself. He sees that signature of Himself on the inside of us. Now do you think it's possible for God to not love Himself? No. Perhaps this is why His love for us goes on and on and on. God is steadily at work, revealing Himself to the world through us.

Earlier we discussed how many of us find it easy to say that we love God, yet we overlook the very signature or trace of God that He has placed on the inside of us. How different it would be if tomorrow you woke up and all that you saw when you looked at people was the image of God? In Matthew 5:8 (NKJV), Jesus said "Seeing God" was a result of having a pure heart. I've often wondered if maybe seeing God had something to do with seeing Him in other people and seeing Him in the situations around us. The Bible says that "To the pure, all things are pure" (Titus 1:15 NIV). Can you see the connection? This is how God loves us. He sees us in His image. This is how we should love ourselves seeing ourselves in His image. This will determine how we love others.

It takes a perfect love to love someone perfectly. Being loved perfectly will perfect and purify the heart of the one being loved. A perfected and purified heart will cause one's "true self" to manifest. Out of the overflow and abundance of this love that is being experienced, this heart develops the ability to love others perfectly, purely, and sincerely. This heart will also develop an all-consuming love for the One who initiated the cycle. This all-consuming love will begin to look for traces of that One, who first loved them, in everything that it comes into contact with. The purity of the perfected heart becomes the lens or filter through which the perfected heart sees the world, putting this person in a position to see things and spot things that any other person would never recognize, at the same time, enabling this person to see past things others would never be able to discard. The lens of this type of love can see past sins. It can see past faults and failures. It sees deep inside the most hidden parts of a man and recognizes the fingerprint of God on the inside of that other individual. It sees the desire of that fingerprint to be awakened, connect to the source of Love, and begin the love cycle.

Sound crazy? It shouldn't. Many of us recognize the fairy tale love stories about how two people fall in love. The initiator begins to love every part of the person they've fallen in love with, giving them permission to be themselves. The one receiving all of this new love and attention can't help but show this person loving them more and more of who they really are, as opposed to putting up the mask that they've used on everyone else. Both participants start to do things they've never done before as a response to this new love.

Women that never thought about cooking all of a sudden find themselves looking up recipe's, watching cooking shows, or calling up Grandma for that old family secret, just so they can do something for their lover. Men that rarely shave or give little attention to their own personal hygiene discover scented deodorants and magically realize that they've been passing a barber shop for months and never even noticed it. She will turn on the radio and every love song reminds her of her lover. Every sweet fragrance brings the other one to mind. When she gets with her girlfriends, she can't help but talk about her man. She hopes that their men love them the way that she's experiencing love from the man who loves her. Love is reciprocated one to another.

This new "high" begins to affect not only the one being loved, but it has an impact on how they treat those around them. If, for example, she receives a bouquet of flowers at work, it brightens up her day so much that she finds it easy to be nice to people that she'd normally want to rip apart. Because of this love that is being experienced, the individual being loved is not going to allow anyone or anything to "rain on their parade". Love purifies and is all-consuming.

Now, imagine this scenario, the one being loved finds themselves deeply in love with someone who is loving them like they've never experienced love before, loving them in a way that they never felt that they deserved to be loved. The one being loved is humbled by this new found love, but they remember the things that they've done in the past, the experiences that they walked through in other relationships, the disappointments, the broken promises, and the abuse. There is a fear of failure, of vulnerability and being hurt. After every act of love, the one receiving the love finds themselves questioning the motives of the one loving them. They find themselves only allowing parts of themselves to be exposed.

It happens all the time. We self-sabotage good relationships for fear of the unknown. If things are too good to be true, we start looking for anything and everything that our imaginations can cause to be suspect. There is no freedom in such relationships; there is no peace. Look at the self-sabotaging attitude of Adam and Eve in the garden.

"Then the eyes of them both were opened, and they knew that they were naked; and they sewed fig leaves together and made themselves apron like girdles.

And they heard the sound of the Lord God walking in the garden in the cool of the day, and Adam and his wife hid themselves from the presence of the Lord God among the trees of the garden.

But the Lord God called to Adam and said to him, 'Where are you?'

He said, 'I heard the sound of You [walking] in the garden, and I was afraid because I was naked; and I hid myself.'

And He said, 'Who told you that you were naked? Have you eaten of the tree of which I commanded you that you should not eat?" (Gen 3:7-11 AMP).

The moment they developed a consciousness of their sin, as soon as they became aware of their own imperfections, they developed a fear. "We are naked; we can't go before God naked. He'll never accept us as naked. We need to cover ourselves up and hide because He's not going to like us if He sees us this way." Did they know that they had done wrong? Yes. Did they know that God would have been displeased with their failures? Yes, but it is very interesting to me that they recognized their nakedness and used this "self-awareness" as a reason to take actions to cover up something that God had never expressed having an issue with.

"And they were both naked, the man and his wife, and were not ashamed" (Gen 2:25 NKJV).

Adam and Eve had always been naked before God. He accepted this about them. He created them this way. Their sin consciousness caused them to take the action to clothe themselves in leaves and hide from God---actions that He had never required of them, nor asked them to do.

Usually when we self-sabotage a relationship, the consciousness of our own sin causes us to perform actions out of an anticipation of a negative reaction that hasn't even taken place yet. 1 John 4:18-19 states:

> There is no fear in love [dread does not exist], but full-grown (complete, perfect) love turns fear out of doors and expels every trace of terror! For fear brings with it the thought of punishment, and [so] he who is afraid has not reached the full maturity of love [is not yet grown into love's complete perfection]. We love Him, because He first loved us (AMP).

As stated earlier, being loved perfectly will perfect and purify the heart of the one being loved. A perfected and purified heart will cause one's "true self" to manifest. Allowing ourselves to embrace the perfect love of God will remove any need to self-sabotage the relationship. We can trust His love. His love brings a confidence that casts out all doubt and fear. When anyone becomes convinced that they can fully trust in this love, the removal of all doubt and fear, places us in a position to be our true selves.

Being our true self, the self that we were created to be is a liberating place. that is the place where we find our security and safety. it is in operating from this place, that we love others sincerely.

FAITH TO BE YOU

The world is full of locks and keys. Not every key fits every lock, but for each lock there *is* a key. Locked up inside of you is the faith to be the full expression of who you were originally designed to be, however we often do not recognize this faith because we have not yet been pricked by the spur of crisis that forces us into digging deep within ourselves to unlock that faith which has been there all along. Plainly put, until our purpose and identity are challenged, we may not be aware of the faith necessary to be authentic. We naturally and falsely assume that we just are who we are, but at some point we all face an identity crisis that causes us to rethink who we are and what we value most. While it's true that we naturally have the potential to be who we were originally designed to be, these moments of crisis help to clarify who we are at our core and to unlock our untapped potential that would have remained dormant and useless.

Many times the image that you portray as yourself is not your true self but rather an adaptation to your environment and a response to conditions that surround you. Life forces you to change faces or take on masks that may not necessarily reflect your true nature, this becomes problematic when we mistake those masks to be a reflection of our true God-given nature.

Let's say that, since you became an adult, you decided you'd never go back to school. Your whole being was totally against the idea. Then suddenly, "life happens" and you're out of a job. Going back to school doesn't seem as repulsive now as it did before. A couple of years in, you find yourself choosing a major that you enjoy. A few years later, you have a fulfilling new career and you're living out your dreams. Somewhere along the way you realize that this "new you" is what you have desired all along but never believed it to be a possibility. Ahaaaa! We have to let go of the thoughts that we have about ourselves and dare to believe that there is more.

In Matthew 16:24 Jesus is teaching that there is more to life than just the mundane motions that we call living. He said:

> "If anyone would come after me, let him deny himself and take up his cross and follow me. For whoever would save his life will lose it, but whoever loses his life for my sake and the gospel's will save it. For what does it profit a man to gain the whole world and forfeit his soul? For what can a man give in return for his soul" (Matthew 16:25 ESV)

In essence Jesus is saying, that we have to be willing to let go of our normal way of thinking and living. *Losing your life to gain your life* implies that there is a part of you that has to die in order to make room for the part of you that needs to live.

Therefore, your true self requires faith: faith in knowing that God has strategically placed you as a gift to this world. You are a present in the process of being unwrapped much like the caterpillar that transitions into a butterfly from the cocoon. The beauty of the butterfly is a direct result of the *death* of the caterpillar in the cocoon.

Perhaps this process is as simple as naturally maturing or it is a response to crisis. Either way, there is a catalyst that starts this whole process. We find ourselves experiencing discomforts that cause us to move beyond our norm and consider new possibilities. Consider what Moses said in Deuteronomy about a mother eagle and her young: "Like an eagle that stirs up its nest, that flutters over its young, spreading out its wings, catching them, bearing them on its pinions, the Lord alone guided him" (Deut. 32:12-13English Standard Version)

Like God, the mother eagle knows that unless she stirs her nest, her babies will never learn to fly. The stirring is a part of the guidance; it becomes the catalyst that forces a change in their lives. The stirring can be a terrifying experience. We generally gravitate towards people and things that make us comfortable; however, with any great calling comes a great sacrifice. If we truly believe that we are designed to be great, there will be a need for faith. There will be a need to take a leap into the unknown, trusting that God has equipped us with the wings we will need to fly. Consider the following passages of scripture:

"Now faith is the assurance of things hoped for, the conviction of things not seen" (Heb.11:1 ESV)

"So faith comes from hearing, and hearing through the word of God." (Romans 10:17 ESV)

If it requires faith to be your true self, and if faith comes from hearing the word of God, then we can safely assume that the key to unlocking your true self rests on your ability to *hear,* and whose *word* it is that you are listening to.

Have you ever stopped to consider how Jesus knew who He was on this earth? Although we may like to believe that Jesus somehow magically just knew who he was, it would be safer to assume that like Samson, Jesus was told of his assignment by his parents. This is an important point to bring up because his parents heard a word from God and communicated that word of God to Jesus.

Many times the word of God that we receive comes from external sources like our parents, teachers, pastors, friends, or maybe it is just something that we heard someone say on TV or read through a book. Whatever the source, a seed of that word gets planted in your heart.

Jesus invested in this word. At the age of twelve, we see Jesus in the temple watering this seed. Jesus was in constant communication with the father. And we finally see God confirming publically the word that had been planted in Jesus and watered through the years. Matthew 3:16-17 states:

"And when Jesus was baptized, He went up at once out of the water; and behold, the heavens were opened, and he [John] saw the Spirit of God descending like a dove and alighting on Him. And behold, a voice from heaven said, This is My Son, My Beloved, in Whom I delight!" (NASB)

It would also be noteworthy to mention the temptation of Jesus that happens almost immediately after God publicly confirms His true self (Matthew 4:1-11). Three times the devil questioned him in the very area that God had confirmed him. Jesus was who God said He was yet the devil attempted to make him question his true self, in the same way that the devil questioned Eve in the Garden of Eden (Gen. 3:1-5). Adam and Eve were already like God yet the tempter comes to bring doubt to that knowledge. Rather than rely on the Word of God that had already proclaimed them as having everything they needed, they listened to the voice of Satan.

The faith required to be who God designed for you to be, the best possible version of you, will always be attacked by those who would seek to manipulate. Whether they wish to capitalize on your success or enjoy seeing you live a mediocre life, the aim is to keep you from maximizing your potential.

We have all experienced a *satan* (from the Greek word *satanas* meaning *adversary*) in our life who tries to take away from who we are. People have a sad way of trying to keep others from blossoming into their full potential. Do you remember the time when Peter tried to keep Jesus from fulfilling his destiny? (Mk. 8:30-33) Perhaps their motive is intimidation, jealousy or just the uninformed assuming that they know what is best for our lives, but whatever the motive you can be certain of one thing, Haters gonna hate! Sometimes you can be your own *satan*. Our own lack of confidence will cause for us to question the possibility of being all that we were designed to be. Our negative self-image can cause us to be our own worst enemy.

Perhaps it is time for us to respond to some of the *satans* in our life the way that Jesus responded to His:

> "But turning around [His back to Peter] and seeing His disciples, He rebuked Peter, saying, Get behind Me, Satan! For you do not have a mind intent on promoting what God wills, but what pleases men [you are not on God's side, but that of men]" (Mark 8:33 AMP).

Jesus told his disciples, "My meat is to do the will of the father"(Matt 3:16-17). By "meat", Jesus is saying that hearing and responding to the word and will of the father literally defines and sustains his life. Consider how many times we see Jesus going off alone to pray. Jesus was constantly placing himself in a position to get his *definition* from the *Definer.*

THE VALUE OF
THE WHOLE

In Luke's gospel chapter 15:1-7, we find the parable of the lost sheep. Jesus tells us a story that a man had 100 sheep and lost one. The man left the 99 to find the 1. Once he found the one sheep the man threw a party and told everyone about the sheep that he had found. Why so much rejoicing over one sheep; after all, the man still had 99 other sheep? The one was a part of the *whole*. With the one gone, the whole was not complete.

It is important for us to recognize our value as individuals so that we can see our collective value as a whole. God is not just concerned about the one lost sheep. He sees the whole flock as important because they all belong to Him.

If you had a basketball team, you'd want every member of that team to be confident in their talents as both individuals and as a team. Each player wants to play with other players that are just as dedicated and committed to the game as they are. A good coach can take the talents of each individual and fit them together to make a powerful unit.

In Genesis 4, we see the story of Cain and Abel. I once heard the late Archbishop Veron Ashe say, "Cain's sin was that Cain loved God and not Abel". We cannot get so caught up in our sacrifice that we forget to love others. They are made in the image of God in the same way that we are. We are our brother's keepers. Jesus said that, "As you have done to the least of these, you have done unto me". (Matthew 25:40 paraphrased)

In his book titled, *Great Christian Thinkers from the Early Church Through the Middle Ages,* Pope Benedict XIV says of Saint Cyprian, "Cyprian teaches that it is precisely in the Lord's Prayer that the proper way to pray is presented to Christians. And he stresses that this payer is in the plural in order that 'the person who prays it might not pray for himself alone. Our prayer', he wrote, 'is public and common; and when we pray, we pray not for one, but for the whole people, because we the whole people are one." Cyprian went on to say, "The Christian does not say 'my father 'but 'our Father, 'even in the secrecy of a closed room, because he knows that in every place, on every occasion, he is a member of one and the same Body." God is concerned with the individual, because the individual is a part of the whole body.

My recognition of being a part of the whole puts a responsibility on myself to do my part, and be the best me that I can be, not just for my sake but for the sake of the whole body.

A chain is as strong as its weakest link. The time has come for each link to recognize their worth as a strong member of mankind, and collectively we become a strong community--- a community of complete, talented, gifted individuals who all recognize our connection one with another.

A PERSONAL REFLECTION

What a journey! Writing this book has been both a liberating and challenging experience for me.

For many years, I felt that what I saw about God made me more of an outcast in certain circles. Although my perspectives and the way that I thought may have caused for me to not fit in with some people or social circles, the person I was created to be, fit in perfectly with the plan that God had and has for me. God took me to a place of redefining and reintroducing Himself to me, away from the church culture that I grew up in, and away from any previous thoughts or ideas that I had developed. It was out of this new relationship that I was able to truly fall in love with Jesus.

When you truly fall in love with Jesus, worship becomes easy. Talking to Him about everything, and giving thanks in all things, as 1 Thessalonians 5:18 teaches, becomes second nature. Looking for what He may be doing or where He is at work around you becomes a very natural thing.

I am far from perfect and I am still in a place where I need Him, but it is humbling to know that Jesus didn't just save me in order to touch the world. Jesus saved me because of His overwhelming love for me. He saved me because He wanted to. He wanted to show me His amazing goodness and forgiveness. He wanted to bless me with all spiritual blessings. Jesus came for me. As I ponder the sobriety of that statement, I remember that scripture says, "For God does not show favoritism" (Rom. 2:11 New Living Translation).

The same way God feels about me is how He feels about you. How amazing it is that God can love the entire world collectively and individually? Our responsibility is to recognize this love.

His love has nothing to do with what we've done or not done. He loves us because He wants to love us. Loving you makes Him feel good. He desires that each one of us join into a love relationship with Him.

Am I saying that we need to ignore the needs of the world or our responsibilities so that we can focus solely on ourselves? No, but I am suggesting that perhaps we have placed such an emphasis on loving the world around us, that we have not placed enough of an emphasis on loving ourselves. As a result, we give to the world around us from an account that is lacking in funds. We convince ourselves that the feelings of emptiness were to be ignored and that our happiness should come out of seeing other people smile because of what we do for them.

A MEAL FIT FOR A KING

Imagine that you are an accomplished chef known worldwide for your incredible steaks. The personal secretary for the President of the United State calls to inform you that the President will be hosting a dinner for some of the world's most powerful and influential people. He is recruiting you to prepare a meal for his honored guests that will serve as a representation of the strength, wealth and power of the United States. He is fully expecting your best. At the end of your phone conversation, the secretary schedules a time for you to meet with the President to discuss the details of this upcoming event. You are set to meet with the President in exactly 24 hours, and the event will be in 48 hours.

You get off the phone and can hardly contain yourself! You are so excited at the thought that the President has a specialized assignment for you. You immediately start to imagine what you could prepare. You browse through all of your favorite entrees trying to decide on which meal would be right for this occasion. After all, the President wants this to be a representation of the wealth and strength of the United States.

You call your best friends together to help you make your decision. Your friends have mixed reactions about you being chosen for such a task. Some are very supportive and begin to give solid suggestions. Others are a bit jealous and begin looking for every reason to turn down any good suggestion that is made. One of your friends says, "You're known worldwide for your incredible steaks. This has to be the reason why the President requested you. He is expecting you to do the thing that you do best."

Another friend speaks up and reminds you that cooking steaks for a large group of people is going to cost money---lots of it. Purchasing the meat and side dishes to go with it at the level of quality that would be expected is going to cost you more money than what you currently have available to spend. He offers an alternative suggestion. "You can't afford all of that steak on your own, but we can put all of our money together, buy something that is very American, like cans of soup, and we will help you prepare it.

This debate has gone on for hours when you realize that you have missed your appointment with the President. You've spent so much time looking for answers from everyone else that you missed your opportunity to meet with the one who gave you the assignment. What kind of input did he have to offer? Was he going to pay for all of the items necessary to prepare this meal? Was he truly that confident in your abilities?

Realizing that you are running out of time, you panic. From that panic, you decide that the soup idea is quickest, easiest, and the most cost effective based on the resources you have. You rationalize within yourself: "Well I can dress the soup up and make it look and taste special. I'll even add extra spices. This will be ok."

The day comes and you serve each guest their own bowl of soup. Because they are hungry, they appreciate what you produce. Because they are cordial, they thank you for your soup and compliment you on how good of a meal it was.

Despite your success in feeding the people, deep down you know you have done them a disservice. Not only did you not give them your best, you have totally misrepresented your country. All things considered, what you have done should be insulting to the guests, the leader, the American people you represent and to yourself.

The President is furious and disappointed. "Why did you miss our meeting?" he snarls. "What was so important that you were not able to meet with me about the assignment that I picked you for?"

You listen, feeling like a child, not knowing what to say. The President continues, "Had you taken the time to meet with me, you would have known that I would be paying all of the expenses and would have provided you with all of the help to make this a success. Had you met with me, you would have known that the reason I chose you for this job is because I wanted to share with the world the very meal that you and only you are known for."

In our scenario, your failure was in not knowing what you had available to you. The question is true for your life right now: How much do you really have to offer the world? What are you allowing to hold you back from being the best you that you could be? You owe it to yourself and to everyone else to quit pretending to be the weak link in the chain. There is strength in you, greatness. You are not alone. You are the image of God and the resources are provided.

As we allow ourselves to be centered on these truths about who God is, and who we are, we will see the value that we bring to this world. We will see that God designed our value to add to the value of *others*. A collection of strong individuals will produce strong families and strong communities.

THE TEMPLE WITHIN

Read through Haggai 1:1-11 and you will hear God telling Israel the reason why they had not been experiencing long-lasting success, if any at all. Verse 4 says: "Why are you living in luxurious houses while my house lies in ruins?"

God was upset with His people because they had invested the time in building houses for themselves, while His house was a complete and total disaster. 1 Corinthians 6:19 says, "Don't you realize that your body is the temple of the Holy Spirit, who lives in you and was given to you by God? You do not belong to yourself." Now let us look at both verses in light of each other.

As people of faith, we have prided ourselves on large church building funds. We have used our lavish homes to show to the world how "blessed" we are, yet we often times neglect to build the temple of God and the Body of Christ. It is the careful developing of this *inward* temple that sets the stage for the successes or failures we have in our lives. Consider also Matthew 7:24-27:

> "Therefore everyone who hears these words of mine and puts them into practice is like a wise man who built his house on the rock. 25 The rain came down, the streams rose, and the winds blew and beat against that house; yet it did not fall, because it had its foundation on the rock. 26 But everyone

who hears these words of mine and does not put them into practice is like a foolish man who built his house on sand. 27 The rain came down, the streams rose, and the winds blew and beat against that house, and it fell with a great crash."

In this story, Jesus is pointing out that a solid house must be built on a solid foundation in order to withstand the storms and trials of life.

If you've ever been shopping for a house, you know that one of the main things that you will want to consider before making that purchase is the condition of the foundation. Is it cracked? Is it level? The foundation is at the center of the structure and is the most importation piece of the entire house. Much of the structural damage that happens to the house is a result of the condition of the foundation. Would it also be true that much of the damage we have seen in our lives, is a result of the condition of our foundation? Should we be surprised that our churches (the outward temple) are still filled with gossip, strife, division, greed, etc.? The foundation of the church at large is the church as each individual. I am the church. You are the church.

My concern for this generation of believers, is that we have been conditioned to be more concerned with the needs of the Body of Christ at large, and not enough emphasis has been placed on the *temple* in which Christ lives. There must be a call for balance and authenticity. The kind of authenticity that comes when we approach the world confident that being the most complete version of who God created me to be, is the greatest gift that I could ever give to the world.

Till we meet again.

Bibliography

"Culture." Merriam-Webster.com. Merriam-Webster, n.d. Retrieved from http://www.merriam-webster.com/dictionary/culture

"Selfish." *Merriam-Webster.com*. Merriam-Webster, n.d. Retrieved from http://www.merriam-webster.com/dictionary/selfish

Page, Ken. "How To Love Yourself First." *Psychology Today*. May 21, 2011. Retrieved from https://www.psychologytoday.com/blog/finding-love/201105/how-love-yourself-first

Polbelarus. "Veron Ashe - Fire in the Rockies." (1:19:57) YouTube. 2014. Accessed April 17, 2016. https://www.youtube.com/watch?v=oovSdVOHyA

Benedict, XIV. *Great Christian Thinkers: From the Early Church through the Middle Ages*. Minneapolis, MN: Fortress Press, 2011.

"Satanas." Strong, James. (1923) *The Exhaustive Concordance of the Bible: Showing Every Word of the Text of the Common English Version of the Canonical Books, and Every Occurrence of Each Word in Regular Order; Together with A Comparative Concordance of the Authorized and Revised Versions, including the American Variations; Also Brief Dictionaries of the Hebrew and Greek Words of the Original with References to the English Words*. New York: Methodist Book Concern.